Bat   r,
d
Tamar

Encountering three women
with messed-up lives

JULIA JONES

ERIES EDITOR: SIMON J ROBINSON

DayOne

© Day One Publications 2008
First printed 2008

978–1–84625–141–2

British Library Cataloguing in Publication Data available

Published by Day One Publications
Ryelands Road, Leominster, HR6 8NZ
Telephone 01568 613 740   FAX 01568 611 473

email—sales@dayone.co.uk
web site—www.dayone.co.uk

Designed by Steve Devane and printed by Gutenberg Press, Malta.

Can there be hope and healing for victims of sexual abuse? God's Word says 'Yes!' In this book, Julia Jones brings timeless lessons from the lives of three Bible women and shows how God's wonderful grace can reach into situations of pain and despair.

Sharon James

Many a Bible reader would gloss over these distasteful episodes in Bible history. Julia Jones demonstrates that they have much to teach an age in which every sexual taboo has been broken and the consequent chaos and dysfunction is commonplace. This readable book offers an understanding of failure and shame which is biblical, God-centred and empathetic.

Ann Benton

Dedication

For Jane, an example of God's transforming grace

Contents

6

These three women had lives that they would not have chosen. Men with double standards brought them much pain, as they were all the victims of inappropriate sexual relationships. But God, by his grace, enabled these damaged women to be used for his purposes.

Tamar

1 The in-laws

Genesis 37

People often bring back some strange souvenirs from their holidays, but if you went to visit Egypt, I wonder if you would bring back anything as unusual as the souvenir brought home by one British woman recently. Jane Felix-Browne, a fifty-one-year-old grandmother, was out horse-riding near the Great Pyramid when she met Omar Bin Laden, a son of Osama Bin Laden, whom she subsequently married.[1] Can you imagine the reaction when she told her family about her holiday romance and her plan to marry? 'You can't be serious! Just think what you would be marrying into! Don't you know what kind of a person his father is?'

These things could very easily have been said to Tamar, although, unfortunately for her, there does not seem to have been any such caution exercised by her family.

SKELETONS IN THE CLOSET

We first meet Tamar in Genesis 38. This is around the time when Jacob is mourning for his son Joseph, who is 'missing, presumed dead'. It is worth gaining some understanding from chapter 37 about the incidents surrounding Joseph's disappearance in order to discover something about the characters involved, as this family will soon be Tamar's in-laws.

If it were not for Reuben and Judah, Joseph (of the coloured-coat fame) would be murdered by the rest of his brothers, as this is their original plan, Plan A, as Genesis 37:20 shows clearly: 'Come now, let's kill him.'

Plan B is then hatched. Reuben suggests leaving Joseph in a dry cistern and allowing 'fate' to take over. In the hot climate, this could well result in an awful death from dehydration and exposure to the elements.

Plan C is Judah's suggestion. This plan is only slightly better, being seen as 'the lesser of two evils': it means only that Joseph will not be murdered or left to die. The calculating Judah has seen a business opportunity as a caravan of Ishmaelites, loaded with all sorts of desirable objects, is passing their way. Judah shows less concern for his brother's welfare than for his own opportunity for material gain. His Plan C is to sell Joseph to these merchants. He gives his brothers two reasons why this will be the best plan: it means that they will not have the burden of Joseph's death on their consciences, and they will also gain twenty shekels of silver. We have to recognize that Judah's real concern is not so much to save his brother from death as to save himself from guilt and, even more appealing to him, to profit materially from the whole transaction.

Sadly, even in our world today, human trafficking is still a reality. It is frequently brought to our attention with high-profile cases such as the tragic deaths of the twenty-one Chinese cockle pickers who were killed in Morecambe Bay in

February 2004. These workers had been receiving just eleven pence an hour in payment for the work that led to so many deaths. Tearfund states, 'Approximately 4,000 individuals are trafficked into the UK each year for the purposes of enforced prostitution.'[2] When we hear such statistics, we are appalled that anyone should gain in such a way from another's misery, especially from that of a family member. But gaining from Joseph's misery is exactly what we see Judah doing here. We have no record of Judah getting any assurances from the merchants that Joseph will be cared for or that no harm will come to him. Instead, we see the wily Judah making sure that he personally gets the best out of the situation. The brothers take Judah's lead, but this is not surprising when we read the description of him in 1 Chronicles 5:2 as 'the strongest of his brothers'.

ECONOMICAL WITH THE TRUTH

It is worth noting that Plan C is not carried out with the knowledge of all the brothers. Genesis 37:29 shows that Reuben knows nothing of this plan: 'When Reuben returned to the cistern and saw that Joseph was not there, he tore his clothes.'

Reuben has been away from the cistern where Joseph had been left, perhaps grazing some of the sheep a little further away. When on his return he goes to check on Joseph, he is utterly dismayed. It was Reuben's plan to leave Joseph in the cistern so that Joseph could later be freed and returned to their father. We see this clearly in Genesis 37:22, where Reuben says, 'Don't shed any blood. Throw him into this cistern here in the desert, but don't lay a hand on him.' The text goes on to say that 'Reuben said this to rescue him from them and take him back to his father.'

It is clear that Reuben is on his own when he makes the discovery of the empty cistern, as we see him then returning to his brothers in a state of distress. It seems that Judah and the others choose not to let Reuben in on the truth. They know that Reuben is compassionate and will insist on chasing after the merchants and buying Joseph back. Allowing Reuben to think that Joseph has been taken away by a wild animal, Judah and the others complete their deceit by taking Joseph's coat— his 'ornamented robe' (37:32), that symbol of their father's favouritism—and dipping it in blood so that their father will believe that Joseph is dead. It is easy to imagine the brothers taking pleasure in defacing this garment that speaks so much of the inequality in their family.

We see Judah's motives here as evil and selfish, but, incredibly, his actions actually result in Joseph's life being saved. With hindsight, Joseph later appraises those actions in the following way: 'You intended to harm me, but God intended it for good' (Genesis 50:20).

WATCH YOUR BACK!

Judah was a main player in what was essentially an evil plan and it is Judah's family into which Tamar is to marry. Sometimes a prospective bridegroom is light-heartedly advised to look at his bride's mother to see what his wife might be like in a couple of decades' time; Tamar should have been advised to take a good look at her prospective father-in-law's character before agreeing to marry into this family! What we have seen of Judah is a man with few principles who is willing to deceive and do wrong if it suits his purposes. He is willing to jeopardize relationships in the family when there is a chance of financial gain and an easy way to be rid of a large irritation. Judah is definitely not the sort of man to trust with your life—or even your pet goldfish! If the chance came to convert your beloved pet into cash, you could well return from your holiday to find an empty bowl with the explanation that Goldie has gone to 'a better place'.

BUT NOT A TOTAL WRITE-OFF

Having said that, and having highlighted the undesirable nature of much of Judah's character, we cannot ignore Jacob's blessing for Judah recorded in Genesis 49:8–12. It speaks of Judah's power and strength, his prowess as a warrior and him gaining the respect of his brothers. It announces the fact that, from Judah's family, the royal tribe will come. Here we see the work of a God of grace. In spite of his powers to deceive and the other sins that we will be discovering, it is from Judah's family that Jesus would descend. This is alluded to in Genesis 49:10: 'the obedience of the nations is his'. The earlier part of this verse points even more clearly to Jesus: 'until he comes to whom [the sceptre] belongs'. It seems surprising to us that the promise of such great things in this blessing comes to Judah rather than to Reuben, the firstborn, or even Joseph, the son who was evidently favoured by both his father and God. For Tamar, with all that she had to endure, it must have brought comfort that, however difficult her experiences were, she was part of this chosen family.

FOR FURTHER STUDY

1. Study the life of Joseph after he was sold into slavery: he became a servant, but was thrown into prison for doing the right thing and resisting Potiphar's wife's advances (Genesis 39:13–20). Despite his innocence, he was held in jail for two years before his skill as dream-solver was remembered. He was then promoted to prime minister, gaining all the power that this entailed (Genesis 41:41–57). His brothers eventually came before him and he had the power to punish them (Genesis 50:15–18). How was it that he was able to respond to them with the words of Genesis 50:19–21?

2. Can you think of other times in the Bible when things have appeared to be going badly wrong, and yet when God has been proved to have been working all things for good all along? (Think, for example, of the account of Esther, and of the life of Jesus.)

TO THINK ABOUT AND DISCUSS

1. Are there any situations in your life that you would not have chosen but can now see that 'God intended … for good'?

2. What difficult situations have you faced when you have not been able to see God's purpose? How can we encourage ourselves (and others) to trust that God is in control even in these situations?

Notes

1 *The Times*, 11 July 2007, p. 3.
2 www.tearfund.org/Extra/Freedom+Day/Slavery+in+our+back+yard.htm (accessed April 2008).

2 'I do'—but perhaps I shouldn't

Genesis 38:1–11

A friend was recently telling me about the arranged marriage of an orthodox Jewish couple. The sixteen-year-old bride-to-be was brought into a room, accompanied by her mother and the groom's mother, to meet her groom, who was accompanied by both fathers. They spent a short time together. The next time the bride set eyes on her groom was at the wedding ceremony itself. After the marriage, she was taken away to have her head shaved—this was how her head would remain for the rest of her life. She then returned to the reception wearing a wig that had been made to appear exactly like her own hair.

This may all seem pretty strange to us; most of us in the West probably cannot imagine entering into marriage with a partner chosen by our parents, although there are some who would say that this is the best way for a partner to be found. We might think that this—especially the head-shaving—is pretty traumatic and may be unable to imagine such a wedding scenario. But if we read Tamar's story, we will recognize that the situation could be much worse.

NOT AS HE WOULD HAVE PLANNED

By the time we get to Genesis 38, Judah has gone to lodge in Adullam with a Canaanite family. No doubt he cannot bear to see his father continue to mourn Joseph, the favoured son, and refuse to be comforted. With Joseph gone, Judah has surely expected Jacob to be more interested in him, but Jacob is too overwhelmed with grief to take much notice of anyone. What seemed such a good idea at the time now just seems to be a big mess. The brothers will certainly be happy to heap the blame for their father's grief and their own guilt onto Judah.

Whichever combination of reasons drives Judah to move away from his father's household, he is still very much a family man: he is a husband and the proud father of three sons: Er, Onan and Shelah. As the father, it is his role to find wives for these sons, so he makes a start with his eldest son, Er. This is where Tamar enters the story, as she is that chosen wife: 'Judah got a wife for Er, his firstborn, and her name was Tamar' (Genesis 38:6).

ENTER TAMAR, AT LAST!

We know hardly anything about Tamar's background: about who she is or where she comes from. It is safe to assume that she is not a Canaanite, as Shua, Judah's wife, is clearly identified as a Canaanite but Tamar is not. In this, we have to say that Judah gets it right for his son, even though not for himself. Both Abraham and Isaac had been concerned about intermarrying with the Canaanites; in Genesis 24:3, Abraham says, 'I want you to swear … that you will not get a wife for my son from the daughters of the Canaanites, among whom I am living.' Isaac said the same thing very plainly to Jacob: 'Do not marry a Canaanite woman' (Genesis 28:1). So perhaps Judah has learnt from his mistakes and determined to get the right kind of wife for his son. His problem, however, is not simply about having the right kind of wife, but having the wrong kind of son.

WHAT HAVE I DONE?

What kind of husband has Tamar said 'I do' to? Sadly, as we read about this family, we see some 'like father, like son' similarities, characteristics that seem to be taken to another level in the sons. Er is described as 'wicked in the LORD's sight' (38:7). This statement is, in effect, Er's epitaph: God puts him to death because of his wickedness. It is actually an epitaph that will, in time, also be appropriate for the second son, Onan—an epitaph we see repeatedly since the time of the Flood, when we read, 'The LORD saw how great man's wickedness on the earth had become ... So the LORD said, "I will wipe mankind, whom I have created, from the face of the earth"' (Genesis 6:5,7).

When we think about Tamar entering into this marriage, we have to recognize that it is pretty unlikely that she has any option other than to say 'I do'. The marriage is most probably not a love-match but simply an arrangement made between Judah and Tamar's father for reasons to which we are not privy, rather like the Jewish marriage we considered at the beginning of this chapter.

So Er and Tamar are married—although not for long. In just two verses we read that they are married and that the Lord then puts Er to death, resulting in Tamar, probably still a very young woman at this time, becoming a widow.

NOT WHAT SHE WOULD EXPECT

This is a tragedy in anyone's eyes. Perhaps Tamar has just

begun to adjust to life with Er, even though it cannot be easy or pleasant to be married to one so wicked. But the greatest tragedy for Tamar is that Er dies before she has conceived a child. It is expected of Tamar that she should produce a child who will carry on Er's family name and line. At this point, Judah suggests the solution that is expected in their society. The second son, Onan, is to have sex with Tamar until a child is produced who can carry on Er's family line (v. 8). This is a type of serial monogamy for Tamar, and not at all what she would have expected when, as a young bride, she married Er.

It is easy to see that this is not a good time for Tamar or for Onan. Tamar must feel like a brood mare, not valued for herself but only for her potential to bear a child. No doubt conditioned by society's expectations, she would be longing for a child. But to Tamar this must seem an awful way to have to go about achieving this goal. So Tamar is far from happy. Her unhappiness about the whole situation is matched by Onan's. He has no desire to father a child for his brother, so he uses that most basic method of contraception, spilling his semen so as not to impregnate Tamar (v. 9). Fathering a child for your brother seems a pretty sordid thing to do, but it was what society expected. This accepted practice was known as levirate marriage and was designed so that the dead brother would have a child to carry on his name. Onan could get out of this obligation, although he would be looked down on for so doing, so instead he goes along with it, wanting the pleasure of sex without the responsibility that should accompany it.

What Onan does in secret is seen by God and is displeasing to him (v. 10). So, as with Er, God puts him to death for his wickedness. We, too, need to recognize that what may be unseen by others is nevertheless seen by God.

KEEP A CLEAR CONSCIENCE

Recently when popping into a shop, I needed to get a 'Pay and Display' parking ticket. A fellow driver kindly offered me his ticket that still had some time left on it. But such tickets have the words 'not transferable' written on them. This was not only a temptation, but also an embarrassing situation. Some evangelists might have seen it as a gospel opportunity; I did not, so what did I do? Did I reject the ticket and cause offence? No; what I did was, I suppose, somewhat cowardly. I took the ticket, sat in the car until the other driver had gone, put the ticket in the bin and bought another one. Some would laugh and believe this to be foolish, but we need always to keep in mind that our Lord sees and is offended by our wrongdoing.

As David says to God after his adultery with Bathsheba, 'Against you, you only, have I sinned and done what is evil in your sight' (Psalm 51:4). Thankfully, we do not have to fear God punishing us with death, but we do need to be aware that, when we sin, the closeness of our relationship with God is affected. One of the most worn pages in my Bible is at 1 John 1; verse 9 says, 'If we confess our sins, he is faithful and just and will forgive us our sins and purify us from all unrighteousness.'

GOD SEES ALL

While it is good to recognize that God sees the wrong that we might feel tempted to 'get away with', it is even more encouraging to see that God sees the wrong done to us. When we face evil, injustice and abuse, when we feel so alone, we need to recognize that there is One who sees, who feels our pain, who weeps for our suffering. Yet our Father God is not an impotent spectator of our pain but is the One who will hold all men accountable for what they have done.

WILL HE DO THE RIGHT THING?

We return to Judah, who is faced with a problem. It is his responsibility to make sure that his dead son has an heir to carry on his name, but now he has only one son left, the youngest, Shelah. We do not know how old Shelah is, but he is obviously still too young to father a child. So Judah suggests to Tamar that she return to her father's home until Shelah is old enough (v. 11). No doubt this is an attractive proposition for Tamar. She would have been quite young when she had to leave home to marry. Life with the in-laws has been far from happy—'traumatic' would be a pretty apt description. So she goes home willingly, glad to be out of this gloomy household for a time. But life is not going to be comfortable for her as a widow with no children in a society that values carrying on the family line so highly.

OUT OF SIGHT, OUT OF MIND

No doubt Judah also breathes a sigh of relief as Tamar packs her bags and leaves. Whatever he says about waiting for Shelah to grow up, he has no intention of letting this woman, who, he probably believes, has brought this double tragedy on his household, near his family again. As time passes, this is borne out by what we read in verse 14: Shelah has grown up, but Tamar has not been given to him as his wife. This could be pretty much the end of the story for Tamar: living in her father's house as a widow, a misfit in society, and even in her own home, with the prospect of never getting out of her situation. But if we have got the impression that Tamar is always going to have her life mapped out for her by her father and father-in-law, we've not seen everything of the strength of character and determination of this young woman.

FOR FURTHER STUDY

1. Read Psalm 51 and its background in 2 Samuel 11–12. How is David feeling as, in the psalm, he reflects on past events? What does he say he will do? What does he want God to do for him?

2. Read 1 John 1. Note that this is addressed to Christians (see v. 3). Is it possible for a Christian to live without ever sinning? How should we respond to God when we have sinned?

TO THINK ABOUT AND DISCUSS

1. What situations do you face when you might be tempted to do something that would displease God but is acceptable to many around us? How does asking the question 'What would Jesus do?' help in such situations?

2. How does it help to know that in times of hurt and abuse, God is with you and feels your pain?

3 A plan conceived

Genesis 38:12–23

Tamar has been living in a state of limbo in her father's house. We do not know for exactly how long this has been going on, but verse 12 describes it as 'a long time'. How must she feel as the months and years roll by? She is no longer the carefree young girl who originally left her father's house, nor is she the wife and mother that she expected to be by now. Does she have brothers and sisters who have married and started producing children? Do these children come to visit and be fussed over? Does she have to show delight in her nephews and nieces while keeping her own pain to herself? Tamar has, however, been holding onto a small ray of hope in the promise made to her by Judah that, when Shelah grows up, he will be able to father a child for her and her dead husband.

But then she hears that Judah is not to be trusted; he has gone back on his word. Shelah has grown up, but she has not been given to him; perhaps Tamar even hears that he has been married to someone else. The small hope that she has had is shattered and it appears that all that the future holds is for her to remain a childless widow, living under sufferance in her father's house.

It would be understandable if she now spirals into a state of depression and becomes a shadowy, withdrawn figure in the household, an embarrassing family member without a defined role. But not Tamar; she is not going to allow herself to become a kind of pitied, Miss Haversham-type of character, as portrayed in Dickens' *Great Expectations*. She hears that her father-in-law is going to be passing nearby and she hatches what can only be described as a desperate, last-chance plan.

THE POWER OF DISGUISE

Tamar dresses up for the part. First, she removes her widow's clothes (v. 14), probably a strange experience after wearing them for so long. I read once about a woman who had been a nun for many years; she found that, when she left the order, wearing ordinary clothes was almost frightening, as she had been hidden and anonymous for so long in her nun's habit.[1] The ex-nun's friends assured her that no one would recognize her for what she had once been and I am sure that this was also true of Tamar. In one of Agatha Christie's mysteries, the killer dresses in the uniform of a waiter and no one sees beyond the uniform. So Tamar exchanges one 'uniform' for another. She dresses herself conveniently in a veil, the apparel of a shrine-prostitute. Surely in her thinking is the thought that she has already been forced to act like a prostitute with her brother-in-law, so this is just one step further. By now, she probably has a rather low opinion of herself, given all that she has been through. It is worth noting that Tamar has obviously got to know Judah's character pretty well, as her plan is a 'honey trap' into which she is sure he will walk.

DESPERATE MEASURES

Tamar is in position by the side of the road, dressed like a prostitute (v. 14). Judah, now a widower, sees Tamar and asks to sleep with her, promising a young goat in payment. As he has not got the goat with him, Tamar asks for a pledge to guarantee payment, suggesting his seal with its cord, and his staff. When she has got what she wants, Tamar allows Judah to sleep with her (v. 18). Tamar has become a cunning and calculating young woman; she is willing to go to such extremes to get the child that she so longs for, the child that will transform her place in society. The bonus of this plan is that Tamar also gets retribution on Judah. She has no desire for the goat that is promised to her but gets what she wants: she is pregnant and she has proof of the identity of the father. She changes back into her widow's 'uniform' and resumes her place in her father's house. When she knows for sure that she has achieved her aim and is definitely pregnant, she surely feels a quiet satisfaction. She is safe in the knowledge that this time she has got the upper hand over Judah, even though in following this course of action she is endangering her own personal safety—she could be burned to death as punishment for prostituting herself.

RIGHTEOUS IN HIS OWN EYES

Judah, however, remains in the dark. He has had his pleasure and is willing to pay, so he sends his friend with the young goat to find the 'shrine-prostitute' and to retrieve the personal items he left as a pledge (v. 20). The casual way in which he lets his friend know of his actions shows something of the immoral state of the society at the time. His attitude seems to be, 'I'm a widower, I have needs, I'll use a prostitute.' He must be somewhat confused when the report comes back that there is no shrine-prostitute in the area. However, it is not the kind of thing to make a big fuss over and no doubt he would rather keep his liaison with a prostitute out of the public arena. It is somewhat like the actor Hugh Grant's 1995 encounter with the prostitute Divine Brown, which caused Hugh Grant extreme embarrassment when it was revealed. Interestingly, Divine says she loves Hugh Grant, as so much good came out of the publicity. She now has the finances to send her daughters to a private school, has a new house and a number of cars including a Rolls Royce![2] Judah, however, is probably simply rather irritated that he has lost his personal seal and staff—but not as sorry as he will be in three months' time! He even sounds quite self-righteous as he states that he has done the right thing by trying to send the goat (v. 23).

It is amazing how easily we are able to belittle our own sin. A few years ago, my family suffered a break-in, when a desk with all its contents was taken. We did keep some rather unusual things in it, such as a camera and binoculars. As we filled out our insurance claim, our concern was to remember correctly all that had been in the desk, but some acquaintances advised us to fabricate the claim so that we could profit from it. The attitude was 'what the insurance company does not know about will do them no harm'. But we knew that to cheat in this way would be an offence against God. This was an easy sin for us to see, but what about all the smaller temptations to do wrong, to cheat the system—'It is only a white lie, it will not harm anyone' or similar self-justifications? Judah allows his encounter with the prostitute to slip to the back of his mind—but not for very long!

FOR FURTHER STUDY

1. Read Matthew 7:1–5. How does Jesus compare our ability to see our own sin with the perception we have of the sin of others?
2. Philippians 2:1–11 is a passage that highlights the humility of Christ. How do these verses, in particular verse 3, help us to have a right view of our sinfulness?

TO THINK ABOUT AND DISCUSS

1. Are you prone to belittle your sin? Are there particular areas in your life where you know you are more likely to overlook your sin?
2. What makes us more aware of our sin? Are there practical steps you can take in your life to avoid becoming complacent about sin?

Chapter 3 Notes

1 **Karen Armstrong,** *Through the Narrow Gate: A Nun's Story* (London: Flamingo, 1995).
2 *The Week*, no. 621 (7 July 2007), p. 10.

4 A plan comes together

Genesis 38:24–26

When a woman is in the early stages of pregnancy, she often chooses to keep it quiet, often not making it public until the first three months, with their heightened risk of miscarriage, are over. However, this is not always an easy thing to do. Early in my marriage, before we had children of our own, a troubled young woman used to spend a lot of time in our home. After a while, she seemed always to be extremely tired, dropping off to sleep if she sat down. We'd been attending a slimming group together, but each week she was gaining weight. Other young people told us about their concerns for her, as she had fallen asleep when they were out together for the evening. I'm sure that if we had had some first-hand experience of pregnancy, we would have read the signs earlier, before it became so obvious that even we were unable to miss it!

A WELL-KEPT SECRET—BUT NOT FOR LONG

We do not know for how long Tamar chooses to keep her pregnancy quiet. Perhaps she reaches the point where her morning sickness can no longer be explained away, or where whoever is in charge of the laundry notices that Tamar has not been having her periods. Or perhaps Tamar just decides that this is the time to reveal her pregnancy herself. The consternation and uproar must be great. To all appearances, Tamar has been living a celibate life in her father's household, yet now she is pregnant! Pregnancy for Tamar is what her family has been longing for—but not like this. We also do not know if Tamar reveals that she has acted as a prostitute or if this is simply the conclusion to which the wagging tongues jump.

IT TAKES TWO

Judah is told that Tamar is guilty of prostitution and is now pregnant (v. 24). In a self-righteous outburst, he demands that she be brought out and burnt for her crimes. Does any guilt gnaw at him as one who has used prostitutes? Does his conscience bother him for his hypocrisy? If it does, he manages to ignore it; he wants to be seen as one who does what is right. It is interesting that, despite Tamar having lived for so long in her father's house, her father-in-law still has so much power over her.

But as she is led out to be condemned, Tamar plays her trump card. Perhaps she has kept the seal, cord and staff hidden in her clothing, for now she brings them into the light (v. 25). That light reveals not so much her sin but the sin and hypocrisy of Judah. From all that we have learnt of Judah so far, it has not been easy to think well of him. But at this point he does the right thing. He could have accused Tamar of stealing the personal objects that she now reveals, but he makes no such defence. Instead, he declares that this sinful woman who is about to be burnt is more righteous than himself (v. 26). It is interesting that he does not refer to his part in the prostitution incident, but rather refers to not giving Tamar to Shelah. Living in a society that accepted such different standards for men and women meant that he found it hard even to recognize prostitution as sin. This does not mean that having such double standards is acceptable to God; it is actually something God explicitly condemns in Hosea 4:14: 'I will not punish your daughters when they turn to prostitution, nor your daughters-in-law when they commit adultery, because the men themselves consort with harlots and sacrifice with shrine-prostitutes.'

Judah's failure to keep his word is what seems to be uppermost in his mind. This tells us something of the damage that wilful, unconfessed sin can have in our lives. It gnaws away at us, it accuses us, until it is brought into the light and dealt with by our confessing it to our Father and accepting his forgiveness. Back to that well-worn page in my Bible: 'If we confess our sins, he is faithful and just and will forgive us our sins and purify us from all unrighteousness' (1 John 1:9).

NAME AND SHAME

At last we see a change in Judah. It is a shame that it has taken such extreme circumstances to bring him to this point of recognition of his own sin and, so it seems, to an attitude of repentance. It would be easy to write Judah off for life as a thoroughly bad lot. He has made many wrong decisions, but later he is seen to be humble and caring. Perhaps when Tamar's pregnancy and his part in it become public, he is humiliated and this results in humility born of experience. It is encouraging to see that God does not choose to use only those who have always got it right: he also chooses and uses those who have got much wrong and have learnt hard lessons from such experiences. In fact, God chooses whom he chooses.

Even with Judah, all is not lost; he is not a hopeless, useless case. In Genesis 43–44, we see Judah showing great care and consideration towards his father and brother Benjamin; it is good to see that he has matured into someone who is both responsible and dependable. He volunteers to be kept in captivity instead of Benjamin so as to lessen his father's anxiety: 'let your servant remain here as my lord's slave in place of the boy' (44:33). Also, as one who earlier seemed to try to wriggle out of accepting the blame, he is at that point willing to take the blame for something for which he is not directly responsible: 'If I do not bring him back to you, I will bear the blame before you … all my life!' (44:32). We can see very clearly that the exposure of his earlier guilt has changed Judah for the good.

Perhaps that can be a help to us when we are plagued with regret for past sins and mistakes, those actions for which we would so like to be able to turn back the clock to undo. I firmly believe that, while it is no excuse for sin and wrong choices, no experience we have is wasted as far as God is concerned. If we are willing and will allow him to, God can use even the bad things in our lives for our growth and maturity. He can also use such experiences to give us understanding of and patience with those who go through similar things.

FOR FURTHER STUDY

1. Read Psalm 103. How is the relationship between God and us described here? What does God desire for us with regard to our sin? What has God done with our confessed sin? (See also Micah 7:19.)
2. Read Hebrews 10:19–23. What comfort do these verses give? What are we to do? How might these verses help someone who has been the victim of sexual abuse?

TO THINK ABOUT AND DISCUSS

1. How would you advise someone who has confessed his or her sin to God but still feels guilty about it?
2. If you feel guilt because of past sexual encounters, is it right that you should always feel this guilt? Is there a time when it is wrong to feel guilt?

5 Happily ever after?

Genesis 38:27–30

Most births bring happiness and satisfaction to the parents, family and friends. For Tamar, there is the double joy that she is now a mother and that her time of shame is over: the shame she would have felt as a childless woman in a culture that expected her to produce children as her primary role and responsibility; the shame and awkwardness of being a widow sent back to her father's home and becoming dependent on him again; the shame of how she became pregnant. All of this is forgotten in the euphoria of the birth, not of one son, but two. The description of the birth almost brings tears to the eyes of any woman who has experienced labour and birth, as well as great admiration for Tamar, who did not have the pain relief or medical intervention that is available today! Yet, even in this birth, there are signs of family likenesses, of earlier behaviour that seems to be mirrored in these twin boys.

DOUBLE BLESSINGS?

Jacob, the grandfather of the twins, was the younger of the twin sons of Isaac. But Jacob was determined to have the birthright of the firstborn, Esau. Aided and encouraged by his mother, Rebekah, Jacob stole his brother's birthright and blessing through underhand means (Genesis 25–27). Similarly, as Tamar gives birth to her twins, the one who will be named Zerah, meaning 'scarlet' or 'brightness', puts out a hand as if he will be born first, yet he pulls back his hand and Perez is actually born first. The name Perez means 'breaking out', and he has indeed broken out ahead of his brother to claim all that comes with being the firstborn.

I wonder how aware Tamar is of this. Is she too exhausted by her labour to take any of it in, or does she, at this early stage, recognize that there is likely to be trouble ahead for these brothers? I imagine it is probably the former after such a traumatic labour. As Arthur Rendle Short notes,

'Tamar was fortunate to survive. The midwife must have been a woman of some skill and resource to diagnose correctly such a rare and difficult condition [locked twins], and to bring her patient through successfully.'[1]

It is worth noting that, in Numbers 26:20, where the descendents of Judah are listed, Perez is recorded before Zerah, indicating that he was accepted as the firstborn. The one whose hand made the first appearance was superseded by the one who pushed him out of the way and was born first. No doubt this was a family debate that ran and ran, causing even more friction for this far from peaceful family.

CALL ME MUMMY

So Tamar is the proud mother of Perez and Zerah. Would one twin perhaps perpetuate Er's name and the other Onan's, or would Judah claim them both in his own name? We live in an age of complicated families with step-parents and half-siblings. This family is just as complicated, as Judah, who should have been the grandfather of Tamar's children, is in fact their father. Sadly, we don't know much of what happened next, what domestic arrangement Judah and Tamar came to. Did Tamar now take her place as the wife of Judah? We don't know what was in store for these twin boys, but their births and their names indicate that there might be further heartbreak and family rifts for Tamar to bear. Did Perez continue to be the one who was 'breaking out' against a quiet life? Was Zerah a hot-headed individual? What we do know is that Perez, who broke out to be firstborn, was a direct ancestor of Jesus; his name goes down in history with this role, as recorded in Matthew 1:3.

What a different woman Tamar must have been by the end of Genesis 38 compared with when we met her at the beginning of that chapter! She had left her father's home as an innocent in every way but this was no longer the case after she had slept with three men—two brothers and their father! She may also have been innocent of the ways in which some people and some families behave, if she had grown up to believe that people say what they mean and keep their promises. Now she had sadly learned that not all can be trusted. It is an understatement to say that it had been a hard few years for Tamar. We do not know how she coped with all that she had been through—whether she kept it to herself or had friends who helped her to come to terms with it all. From what we have seen of her, it seems that she saw these obstacles as something to climb on, rather than something to trip her up—and these obstacles were enormous.

JOY FROM PAIN
Now Tamar could take delight in her boys, with all her hopes and dreams for what they might become and what they might

achieve. If she had known what part one of her sons would play in the genealogy of the Messiah, her motherly pride would have known no bounds! By his grace, God had used these circumstances, although they were sordid at times, to bring about his purposes.

We must be wary of believing the devil's lies when he says that God cannot use damaged people. If we feel that we have allowed ourselves to be tainted by our godless behaviour, we need to recognize that God is in the business of changing lives around, of turning bad to good. He took Saul, who was fervent in his desire to destroy God's people, and changed him into a man fervent to proclaim Christ, whatever the cost to himself. In Christ, we are all new creations; past sin and past experiences can be dealt with. If we are responsible for the sin, we can take hold of the truth of 1 John 1:9: 'If we confess our sins, he is faithful and just and will forgive us our sins and purify us ... '

I find the encounter between Jesus and the woman who had been caught committing adultery so helpful in revealing Jesus' attitude in such situations. She was brought to Jesus by those who were more concerned to trap Jesus than promote the woman's welfare. Jesus invited those who were without sin to stone the woman, and the crowd melted away. Jesus' words to this woman show such love, tenderness and acceptance: 'Woman, where are they? Has no one condemned you? ... Then neither do I condemn you ... Go now and leave your life of sin' (John 8:10–11).

Jesus' concern was not to make her pay for past sin, but to free her from it so that she could live her life in the security of his forgiveness.

Those who are damaged by the sin of others need to recognize that God's Word says, ' … if anyone is in Christ, he is a new creation; the old has gone, the new has come!' (2 Corinthians 5:17). God's Word also tells us that it is God who purifies those who are his: ' … let us draw near to God with a sincere heart in full assurance of faith, having our hearts sprinkled to cleanse us from a guilty conscience and having our bodies washed with pure water' (Hebrews 10:22).

For the one who has been abused, there is no need to feel guilt, although many do; but Jesus can help us deal even with such false guilt and allow us to see that he has washed us from any uncleanness that we might feel.

If we have been hurt or abused, we can, in time and with the help of godly counsel, know God's comfort. Then God can use us to help others who are going through similar experiences: 'who comforts us in all our troubles, so that we can comfort those in any trouble with the comfort we ourselves have received from God' (2 Corinthians 1:4).

1. Read about the twins' grandfather, Jacob, in Genesis 25:19–34 and chapters 27–37. Notice the consequences of Jacob's actions in Genesis 27:41–45.

2. Paul is a great example of someone who would never have been expected to be greatly used by God. Read about his anti-God lifestyle in Acts 7:54–8:3. Now read Acts 9:1–28. What happened to enable him to be so used by God?

TO THINK ABOUT AND DISCUSS

1. God uses whomever he chooses, not because of who they are and what they can do, but because of his grace. How can an understanding of this truth be an encouragement to us? How should it help us as we consider others who seem to be greatly used?

2. What bad experiences have you faced in your life? Do you believe that God can use these for his glory? How might this happen? (See 2 Corinthians 1:3–7.)

Chapter 5 Notes

1 **Arthur Rendle Short,** *The Bible and Modern Medicine* (London: Paternoster, 1953), p. 35.

Bathsheba

6 One thing leads to another

2 Samuel 11:1–4

When you hear the word 'spring', I wonder what comes into your mind? Perhaps spring flowers and spring lambs, or maybe the romantic thought of Paris in springtime. For Bathsheba, springtime was 'the time when kings go off to war' (v. 1).

This was the time when the majority of healthy men would have disappeared off the scene, accompanying the king in whichever campaign was being fought at the time. The bad weather was past and it was again possible to travel to take up from where they had left off with their enemies. Jerusalem would have had a different, more feminine and relaxed, feel.

It certainly seems that the beautiful Bathsheba is pretty relaxed when we first meet her, lounging up to her neck in a relaxing bath, no doubt perfumed and enriched with scents and oils. It is one of those occasions when you have the evening to yourself to enjoy a bit of pampering and relaxation: a long soak followed by a good read with some favourite snacks to nibble. This is what Bathsheba has planned to do while her husband, Uriah, is off fighting the enemies of King David. But Bathsheba's evening does not work out at all as she has envisaged.

JUST ONE LOOK

It is springtime and David, as king, should be off fighting with his men; but for some reason, whether because of cowardice, laziness or other duties, he is still at home (v. 1). Perhaps he is the kind of man who is great at initiating projects and getting people motivated, but loses interest once things are up and running. It must be a warm evening, as Bathsheba is bathing on her roof, in the open air, in a sort of hot tub. David has gone to bed but cannot sleep because of the heat. He may well have been sleeping on the roof, as it is so warm. We cannot excuse David being in Jerusalem by saying that he has important matters to deal with there, for, if this is the case, surely he would not be in his bed in the early evening. Now he gets up and goes for what he hopes will be a cooling stroll around his roof (v. 2).

As he is walking, his gaze falls on the naked Bathsheba in her bath. We may think that Bathsheba is being provocative by bathing where she might be seen, but she would expect David to be away fighting with his men. So David sees her and is filled with lust; and, rather than look the other way, he calls a servant to come and take a look so that he can find out who she is (v. 3). David is so taken up with his own desires that he shows no concern for Bathsheba's dignity: his servant is also now gazing on her nakedness. She is identified as 'Bathsheba … the wife of Uriah'.

This should be the point at which David gives a sigh for what cannot be and returns to his bed with a good book. But David makes no effort to resist the temptation he faces. In the full knowledge that she is a married woman, he sends for her so that he can sleep with her (v. 4). His sin is compounded by the fact that, while David is at home enjoying the luxury of his palace and Bathsheba, Bathsheba's husband Uriah is out fighting for David, his king. But David does not allow such details to spoil his pleasure!

DRIVING THROUGH A RED LIGHT

The biggest problem with lust is when we do not, or will not, see the red light, the warning signal that means we should stop when we are tempted. Lust is a common sin for many, whether it is a sexual lust or a lust for other things. But when we are tempted, we must stop at the red light; we must stop and say sorry to God if we have indulged in sin in our thoughts, and ask for his strength to deal with the temptation. At times, it means we must stop before we go where we might be tempted. It is no use praying 'Lead us not into temptation' (Matthew 6:13) if we then watch unhelpful programmes, read unhelpful material, look at unhelpful websites or go to places where we know we will be tempted.

Do you recognize the red lights in your life? For some, it will be the pull of TV soap operas; for others, perhaps reality shows or women's magazines and novels. These can seem harmless, but what are the values we are imbibing as we get taken up with the characters and storylines? In the past, I have found myself so carried along with the action in a soap that I have wanted characters to act in immoral ways; my thoughts have become corrupted and I have recognized the need to give up watching. Alternatively, perhaps the pull of these programmes or other things is such that they dominate our lives to the extent that we would rather spend time on these things than get involved in activities that might help us grow as

Christians or in areas where we might serve. I do not believe that it is necessary totally to give up on such entertainment, but we do need to be really honest with ourselves. If we recognize that through a particular activity we are indeed being 'led into temptation', we must give it up. At one time I could not imagine life without watching soaps, but having recognized their unhelpful influence and the utter waste of time spent watching them, I can now say that I do not miss them at all.

And what about the temptation of materialism? What makes you want more and more? Are you a slave to labels—valuing yourself by how much you spend on various things? We need honestly to answer such questions. I cancelled the mail-order catalogues I used to receive, as I found that there were many things I 'really needed' yet which I would happily have existed without if I had not seen them advertised in the catalogues.

For many women, though, perhaps one of the greatest temptations is in the area of our tongues. Gossip is so easy to fall into: the criticizing and judging of others, saying things that we would never say face to face. This is hard to tackle; it creeps up on us mid-conversation and comes so easily into our minds. We need to be tough and not allow ourselves to be drawn in. When we think of something we would like to say in criticism of another, we must make the choice not to speak it but silently to confess that sin to God. I have to admit that this is still a 'work in progress' in my life.

But back to David. Did he know, as he made his way up onto his roof, that he was likely to see such a scene? If he did, he should not have gone there. Or, if he took this evening stroll in all innocence, he should have turned away, not kept gazing. Sadly, however, he did not make such a wise choice. After looking and lusting, he compounded his sin by acting on the wrong desires that had been stirred up within him. Fully aware that Bathsheba was a married woman, he sent for her, not so that she could keep him company or give him news of how her husband and the troops were doing, but for sex. He sent for her so that his lust could be satisfied. He drove on through the red light, fully aware that to do so was wrong and that such action could lead to disaster.

SIN CORRUPTS

So David sends for Bathsheba. Does she have a choice? Can the wife of an ordinary soldier refuse the demands of the king? No—David uses his position to take what he wants. His intention is not to form a lasting relationship with her: he takes what he wants and sends her home (v. 4). As far as he is concerned, it is simply a one-night stand, a pleasant distraction when he is at a loose end.

How must Bathsheba have felt? It is most likely that she felt a mixture of emotions that would later run along the lines of 'If only … ' and 'Why me?' What she had planned to be a relaxing evening of pampering had turned into a nightmare; she had been summoned from her own home and used like a prostitute by David. After the cleanness of her bath, she would now feel the uncleanness of adultery, feeling that she had betrayed her husband who was fighting honourably for the very man who had abused her. Her sense of shame would be enormous, through no fault of her own; her regret for choosing to bathe on the roof would be immense, plaguing her with false guilt; and no doubt she would feel that she had reached the depths of despair—yet the worst was still to come!

FOR FURTHER STUDY

1. David was a man with a great reputation, from the time when, as a young man, he killed Goliath (1 Samuel 17:20–58) to his upright behaviour when Saul pursued him, seeking to take his life (1 Samuel 26:7–11). People spoke well of him—in 1 Samuel 29:3–11, he is even compared to an angel. This is the man God chose to rule his people. Why do you think this godly man fell into temptation in this way?
2. Bathsheba would have felt great shame and guilt. Was she right to feel like this? Discuss your answer.

TO THINK ABOUT AND DISCUSS

1. Are there people you look up to and who you believe could never sin? How should you pray for such people?
2. Identify the area in which you feel the greatest struggle with sin. Pray about this. What practical steps can you take to avoid this temptation?

7 Oh, what a tangled web we weave, when first we practise to deceive!¹

2 Samuel 11:5–25

The number of unplanned and unwanted pregnancies in the UK is very high these days; sadly, many end with abortion, whether through the morning-after pill or a clinical intervention. Such pregnancies are not a new phenomenon. In societies that take the moral stance that pregnancy outside marriage is unacceptable, many different methods are employed to be rid of the embarrassment of an illegitimate child: even just a century ago in the UK, women would be taken into establishments where they would give birth and then have the child taken away for adoption; women in Ireland still travel across to England to have an abortion; many children have grown up believing their grandparents to be their parents, a cover-up of the embarrassment of an older daughter's unplanned pregnancy. But none of these methods is employed by David on Bathsheba's behalf.

BE SURE THAT YOUR SINS WILL FIND YOU OUT

Sex with Bathsheba has been a pleasant distraction on an

evening when David is at a loose end. As noted earlier, David has not planned any long-term involvement with her. But then, a number of weeks later, David receives a wake-up call: Bathsheba is pregnant. Does David even remember Bathsheba and what happened? Perhaps at first he looks for another culprit to blame for the pregnancy; perhaps she has slept with someone else while her husband is away. His advisors would be able to tell him that Bathsheba is an upright woman who does not willingly cheat on her husband; this is not her habit. The Bible makes it clear that she cannot already have been pregnant when David slept with her, as she had just finished purifying herself after her period (v. 4). Her husband Uriah is still away at war, so David, recognizing that the child must be his, comes up with a plan.

A MAN OF PRINCIPLES
David sends for Bathsheba's husband, Uriah (v. 6). This is surely a shock for Uriah: 'Why me? What have I done?' He rushes straight to David and is asked how the war is going. It appears to him that David simply wants news from the battlefield (v. 7). He is surely perplexed, as David has never asked him to bring such information before. Why doesn't David use his usual messengers? No doubt Uriah feels privileged at being trusted to give reliable information to his king. But it is not actually the information that David wants. His plan is to get Uriah back home to his wife so that he can sleep with her and the 'large premature' baby will be born with Uriah's name.

Uriah, however, is a man of principle; he will not allow himself to enjoy home comforts, including a return to the

marital bed, while his fellow soldiers are still on the battlefield
(v. 11). He does not even go to his own house, but sleeps at the
palace entrance (v. 9), showing that at present he is employed
in the king's army, a soldier still on duty.

David is both perplexed and frustrated by the honourable
actions of this righteous man. He thought that bringing Uriah
home would solve the problem of Bathsheba's pregnancy. He
has not reckoned on the fact that others have higher principles
than he has. He certainly feels some sense of guilt when
confronted by Uriah's upright actions. David has already sent
gifts to Uriah; next he seeks to ply him with good food and
drink, banking on the fact that such things will relax Uriah's
principles so that he will go home and sleep with his wife. But
Uriah chooses to spend a second night sleeping on his mat with
David's servants (v. 13). You can imagine David storming
around the palace in a foul temper, kicking the cat, unable to
tell anyone what his problem is. But then there is a ray of light,
as David, ever the optimist, comes up with another plan.

THE DOWNWARD SPIRAL

David has discovered the sad truth that, if we are not willing to
say 'No' to sin, it so often leads to more sin. Now that his plan
of making Uriah believe he is the father of Bathsheba's child
has failed, David sinks lower in his sin. It is as if he is on a
downward spiral but will not recognize it or say 'Enough is
enough'. Uriah is again used as a messenger, but this time he
carries his own death warrant. David orders him back to the
front with a message to Joab the army general that says, 'Put
Uriah in the front line where the fighting is fiercest' (v. 15).

This is bad enough in itself, deliberately placing Uriah in

danger, but David is not leaving anything to chance. The message continues, 'Then withdraw from him so that he will be struck down and die.'

Joab must wonder what wrong Uriah has done to David, how he has offended him. He is unaware of Uriah's innocence and that he himself is about to be the instrument to bring yet more injustice to Uriah. But Joab is a military man who follows orders and respects his king. Whatever unease he feels personally about the situation, he puts it aside and follows David's instructions to the letter. He places Uriah in the most dangerous place, 'where he knew the strongest defenders were' (v. 16).

This time, David's plan works like clockwork: Uriah is killed. Though not understanding why, Joab recognizes that David will appreciate news of this 'casualty of war' and so mentions Uriah by name as he reports on the latest death toll. It is obvious that this manoeuvre has not been a wise or necessary part of the campaign, since Joab is keen that the messenger explain it fully to David (vv. 19–21). Joab must be feeling rather uncomfortable about this action—it goes against the wisdom of a military strategist—so it is clear that David has also led Joab to take wrong actions, loading him with a burden of guilt that is not his own. One small thing in David's favour at this point is that he does send Joab a message indicating that he must feel no blame for the death of Uriah and other men as a result of his command: 'Don't let this upset you; the sword devours one as well as another' (v. 25). Yet he manages to give this assurance without taking the blame onto himself!

David's evening of pleasure has led to the unnecessary deaths of a number of his men, including the innocent, upright

Uriah. This has all been carried out in an effort to rid himself of the embarrassment of being accused and shamed as an adulterer. It is hard to know how David feels as he receives the news of these deaths; does he feel any tinge of remorse, or is he just pleased to be out of a tight spot?

FOR FURTHER STUDY

1. Read 2 Samuel 12:1–14. How is David eventually brought to his senses and made to recognize the reality of his sin?
2. David wrote Psalm 51 after Nathan the prophet helped him to face his sin. Why do you think he prayed the words of verse 4: 'Against you, you only, have I sinned'?

TO THINK ABOUT AND DISCUSS

1.Was Joab right to obey David's order and place Uriah in such a dangerous position? How should we respond when we feel we are being led into wrong actions?
2. Can you think of times when you have tried to cover up one sin, and ended up committing more sin? What do you plan to do differently next time?

Chapter 7 Notes

1 **Sir Walter Scott,** *Marmion*, canto vi, stanza 17.

8 Widowed, married, bereaved, then a mother!

2 Samuel 11:26–12:25

I sometimes watch the Service of Remembrance for those who have lost their lives in the various conflicts in which the UK has been involved. One of the most poignant moments is when a young widow from a recent conflict takes her place in the parade of those who have been bereaved. It highlights the lasting pain that there will be in her life because she has lost her husband at such a young age.

Bathsheba is in a similar situation. Her husband has gone to war 'in the spring'; no doubt she expected him to return again when the weather became wintry, but now he is dead. Bathsheba must be wracked with guilt and regret but, since our passage contains no indication of any guilt on Bathsheba's part, I believe it is safe to conclude that she was only a party to adultery because she had no choice; yet her innocence does not protect her from the regret that exacerbates her grief.

She must know that Uriah had been back in town but had not come home because he felt it was not the right thing to do. Bathsheba must be going over and over in her mind the question as to whether she could have made things turn out differently. What if she had not chosen to bathe on the roof on that night? Should she have pleaded more with her king not to sin in this way?

Bathsheba is a woman to be pitied: her husband is dead, she is pregnant, and she fears that soon the sympathy she is receiving as a widow will become condemnation because she will be judged to have been unfaithful to her husband. Her tears are many; tears for what happened with David, for the loss of her husband and for what she is yet to face when her pregnancy becomes obvious.

Bathsheba mourns for her husband (11:26); she does not merely observe the set time for mourning, but she grieves for him. Those around her would expect her to grieve, but may be puzzled by the extent of the hopelessness she is experiencing. How soon will their sympathy turn to anger against her? Bathsheba must be expecting condemnation to come her way soon.

TOO GOOD TO BE TRUE

When the time of mourning is over, David sends for Bathsheba so that she can become his wife (v. 27). His second plan has worked out and he can now pass the baby off as extremely premature. There would certainly be whispers and rumours as Bathsheba is married and gives birth to a son so soon after her husband's death, but no one would dare to speak out such suspicions against the king. In fact, this might even be doing David's reputation some good, with people perhaps saying, 'How good David is to show such compassion to this young widow by marrying her, and taking on her unborn child too!' So David feels that he has got away with it, has covered his tracks and escaped the consequences of his sin.

However, as we read in 2 Samuel 12, God is not going to allow David to shrug off his sin so easily. Bathsheba may be able to put aside thoughts of her son's conception and enjoy her newborn, but not for long.

SHORT-LIVED JOY

This marriage is not going to be free from pain and distress. David thought that he could deceive both those around him and God. Nathan the prophet, however, makes David's sin clear (12:7–10) and David and Bathsheba face what is every parent's nightmare: David is told that he will not die for his sin but, worse than that, his newborn son will die (12:13–14).

Bathsheba must feel that there will be no end to her misery. She watches as the prophet's words are fulfilled: her baby becomes ill, her new husband is wracked with guilt, he fasts, goes without sleep and he prays, pleading with God for the life of their son. The desire to cover up the sin of the past is forgotten as anxiety for this young life takes over. It is at this time that David writes Psalm 51, expressing the depths of his repentance and regret. For a week, David and Bathsheba watch as their child worsens, and then he dies. Has Bathsheba understood anything of the events leading up to Uriah's death? Now, just because of David's lust on a warm evening, the lives of two innocent people have been lost. David may repent of his sin, but both he and his wife must suffer the consequences of it. Bathsheba is experiencing the depths of despair and hopelessness; she must wonder whether life will ever be worth living again.

LOVED BY THE LORD

In the midst of his own grief, David shows compassion for Bathsheba. He comes to her and comforts her (12:24). Is this comfort hard to take? If it had not been for David, Bathsheba would still be married to Uriah and would not have experienced the agony of losing a child. It seems, however, that Bathsheba accepts his comfort; she accepts his loving and she becomes pregnant again. This pregnancy is plagued by the fear of losing this child also—might God continue to punish David's sin in this way? When this second son is born, Bathsheba must feel such great anxiety for him that it is very hard to relax and enjoy him. They name him Solomon, meaning 'peace and prosperity', expressing their longing that they will now be able to enjoy a sense of peace with God.

Then the prophet Nathan comes to visit, to bring, not a fluffy teddy bear, but a message of reassurance from God: baby Solomon is also to bear the name Jedidiah, meaning 'loved by the LORD' (12:25). At last, Bathsheba can relax and enjoy her child; she can stop being the understandably over-anxious parent and can become a mother confident in the fact that God is watching over her child. As she watches him grow, she can remind herself that he is 'Peace, loved by the LORD'. She has experienced in her own life the tender touch of a Father God. In years to come, she will also be encouraged that, out of all David's sons, it is Solomon Jedidiah who will follow him as king of Israel.

FOR FURTHER STUDY

1. This incident of the suffering of a child being due to the sin of a parent is a one-off; this is the only time Scripture makes the link. What does Jesus say in John 9:2–3 about the man born blind?
2. Read 2 Samuel 12:20–23. What is surprising about David's reactions following the death of his son? Why does he act like this?

TO THINK ABOUT

1. In 2 Samuel 12:23, David speaks with certainty that he will 'go to' his son again. How are we to understand this? Does it teach us anything about the eternal destination of one who dies so young? Would this have been a help to Bathsheba in her grief over the loss of her son?
2. How might you give support to a bereaved person? Think in terms of practical as well as spiritual help.

9 An ambitious mother

1 Kings 1

When I see pictures of Prince Charles on television, I often feel quite sorry for him. He is not as young as he was and is still waiting to take on the role of king of England, the job for which he has been trained all his life. His mother, Queen Elizabeth II, seems to be, like her mother before her, of the long-living type. I wonder whether Charles ever thinks that the monarchy should have a retirement age—but that could work against him, as his own time in the job could then be very short! But at least he, as the eldest son, knows that he is next in line to the throne.

Things were not so straightforward for the monarchy in Israel. It was the task of the present king, with the advice of God's prophets, to agree who was to be next in charge. In this chapter in 1 Kings, we see that David is now elderly and unwell, so one of his sons, Adonijah, decides to take advantage of the situation and declares himself king. Bathsheba is concerned on two counts: firstly, she believes that her 'loved by the LORD' son is the rightful heir; and secondly, she recognizes that Adonijah obviously sees Solomon as a threat to his reign and will treat him and his mother as criminals once David is dead, their crime being 'plotting against him'. So Bathsheba, with Nathan the prophet's encouragement, goes to plead with David for his help and protection (vv. 11–21).

OH NO, NOT THAT MAN AGAIN!

After Bathsheba has made her case with David on Solomon's behalf, Nathan arrives and is given an audience with David. Bathsheba has to wait outside during this time, no doubt filled with anxiety about what is being said. The first time Nathan spoke about her family, it was to say that the son to whom she had just given birth would die, but now it seems that he is on her side. But can she be sure of this? A chill goes through Bathsheba's heart as she reflects on that past episode, still painful after all these years. But Nathan was also a source of encouragement to her when she, as a young mum concerned whether her next son would live or die, was given the assurance from him that this son was 'loved by the LORD'. So, what is it to be from Nathan today for her and her family? Is he really going to stand with her in helping Solomon to take his place?

Nathan checks with David that he has not told Adonijah that he will rule after him. The passage does not record the rest of this conversation but it is obvious from what follows that David has made no such promise.

MY SON, THE KING!

Bathsheba is called back into David's room and David makes things clear. He repeats the promise that he has made, that 'Solomon your son shall be king after me' (v. 30). He reassures her that, with the support of the prophets and priests, Solomon will be king. Zadok the priest and Nathan the prophet then anoint Solomon in Gihon (vv. 38–39). The proclamation they make is 'Long live King Solomon!'

Solomon then takes his place on his father's throne; he does not need to wait until David is dead because, due to David's ill-health, Solomon will act as regent. News of this reaches the gathering of Adonijah the usurper (v. 41). His supporters are concerned for their own skins and scatter, leaving Adonijah afraid for his life. But Solomon's first ruling as king is hallmarked by the wisdom for which he will become famous: 'If he [Adonijah] shows himself to be a worthy man, not a hair of his head will fall to the ground; but if evil is found in him, he will die' (v. 52).

I wonder how often Bathsheba uses that phrase 'My son, the king'. I can imagine the pride in her voice as she does so. To see him anointed, taking his place on his father's throne and acclaimed by the people fulfils her greatest hopes. As she stands there in her best dress observing it all, even if she does not actually nudge people and murmur, 'My son is the king, you know', surely such an attitude radiates from her face. Then to hear the wisdom of his first judgement, her joy and pride know no bounds. What a long way she has come from the woman who felt that, due to another's sin, she would never be able to hold her head up in respectable society again!

Bathsheba's story is a message to us that no situation, however bad, is ever hopeless if God is involved. The God we worship is the one who can turn even the most difficult situations into something useful for him. He can use those who feel helpless and hopeless in situations over which they have no control. The Messiah was to come from David's line and could have come through any of David's wives. But it was Bathsheba who was to be the grandmother, many times removed, of Jesus the Saviour (Matthew 1:6). If only she had known this, her comment could have been 'My son is the king—and the ancestor of the King of kings!'

FOR FURTHER STUDY

1. Read 1 Kings 2:1–4. Look at the good advice David gives to his son Solomon as he is about to die. What do you read here that shows that David has learnt from his mistakes?

2. Another mother of a son born for greatness was Mary, the mother of Jesus. Read her outpouring of praise in Luke 1:46–55. How does she express her delight in God's goodness to her?

3. Read the familiar words of Luke 2:1–20. What is Mary's response to all that has been said about her son?

TO THINK ABOUT

1. What would you say to someone who feels that, because of past circumstances, God cannot use him or her? Take lessons from both David as the instigator of sin and Bathsheba as the victim of that sin.

2. If Bathsheba were to write a song of praise to God for the gift of her son, what might she say? Do you always remember to praise God when he brings good out of your dark times?

Tamar

10 Like father, like son

2 Samuel 13:1–7

mnon is his father's son. We have already seen that
David saw Bathsheba and wanted her sexually,
showing no concern for where this action might
lead, and now Amnon is about to repeat this same
act of selfishness. He believes that he has fallen 'in love' with
his half-sister Tamar. But we will see that 'in lust' is a far more
accurate description. He desires her, he thinks about her all the
time, and no one else measures up to her. To be close to her,
but unable to touch her, is torment for him. In fact, it is such
torment that it is making him ill (v. 2).

As David's firstborn son, he is, no doubt, accustomed to using
his prime position in the family to get his own way. He has no
thought of self-control, no willingness to recognize that to
follow through on his desire will cause himself and others
incalculable distress. What should he do at this point? He should
keep himself away from the temptation, take a cold shower, got
involved with an occupation that will absorb him, say 'No' to
his wrong lusts. But, like his father before him, Amnon is used to
getting what he wants. He is used to possessing that upon which
he sets his eyes. It has not been his habit to say 'No' to
temptation, and he is not about to start now.

NOT MUCH OF A FRIEND

Amnon has a friend called Jonadab. In fact, he is not only a friend but is actually Amnon's cousin. Jonadab shows the concern of a true friend when he notices that Amnon is looking downcast day after day. Jonadab cannot understand why Amnon is like this; he is the king's son, after all, with all the luxury and privilege that position brings. No doubt this is a role that Jonadab would have loved for himself: to be the prince rather than merely the prince's cousin.

So Jonadab asks Amnon what the problem is. Amnon replies that it is his love for the unattainable Tamar that is getting him down. At this point, Amnon needs Jonadab to help him to see that his feelings for Tamar are wrong and to help him overcome them, perhaps encouraging Amnon to get involved in some absorbing activity, a hunting expedition or something. But, sadly, this is not Jonadab's response. There is no record of him trying to get Amnon to see the wrongness of his desires; rather he affirms what Amnon already feels: that what Amnon wants, Amnon should have, no matter the consequences.

AN EVIL PLAN

Jonadab comes up with a plan so that Amnon can sleep with Tamar. Amnon is to take to his bed so that, when David his father comes to visit, he will be concerned and ready to give him what he wants. These two cousins know that David is likely to grant any request of this favoured son without thinking too much about the consequences. Yet, as someone who himself has fallen to the temptation of lust, surely David will be careful to guard his son from such temptation? Perhaps

Amnon's description of Tamar as 'sister' stops the alarm bells ringing for David (v. 5), but what should put David on his guard, however, is Amnon's desire to 'watch' Tamar; David should remember the trouble that 'watching' had got him into.

The plan that is hatched between these two cousins is cold and calculating; it shows no concern for Tamar and is definitely not evidence of the love that Amnon claims to have for her. This plot to bring Tamar to Amnon seems to have yet another sinister element to it, no doubt the work of the shrewd Jonadab: David is actually manipulated into putting Tamar in Amnon's way. Might this perhaps be an insurance policy, so that when David hears of what has happened he will find it hard to punish anyone, as his name will be linked with the plot regardless of the fact that he acted in naive innocence?

FOR FURTHER STUDY

1. *Read 1 Chronicles 3. Work out David's family tree. Notice particularly the relationships to one another of Amnon, Absalom and Tamar.*
2. *Read Proverbs 17:17; 18:24; 27:6. What do they teach about friendship?*

TO THINK ABOUT AND DISCUSS

1. *How should we respond when we feel tempted to do something that we know is wrong? How might we seek to avoid giving in to such temptation?*
2. *Do you have good friends who are willing to help you do what is right rather than encourage you in wrong ways? How can you be a good friend to others?*

11 A man's world

2 Samuel 13:8–19

Tamar is getting on with her normal life as a daughter of the king. She has plenty of female companions in a household overloaded with wives, concubines and half-sisters. I wonder how interested in men she is at this time. Is she a bit of a tomboy and totally uninterested? Or perhaps she is dreaming of the day when she will meet her Prince Charming, have a fairytale wedding and live 'happily ever after'.

She is interrupted in the middle of any daydreams she might be having and told to go to her brother Amnon's house. Does she perhaps feel a bit of resentment at having to cook for him, or is she happy to help because her half-brother is ill and she is keen to see him well again? We do not know, but we do observe that Tamar really has no choice.

HE GETS WHAT HE WANTS

At David's instruction, she goes to Amnon's house. In ill-thought-out indulgence for his son, David tells her to go to her brother's personal quarters, something normally unthinkable in that culture. David overturns this norm of society, and Tamar has to go along with Amnon's wishes. She cannot bring a loaf from home or pick one up from the baker's on her way in, but has to knead her dough and bake her bread while Amnon looks on.

She has humoured him so far, but when he then refuses the bread that she offers, she must start to feel somewhat disgruntled (v. 9). After all, she has gone along without complaining with all that she has been asked to do, but Amnon will not eat. He now gives yet another instruction: everyone else must leave, meaning that Tamar is now alone with Amnon. He then demands that she take the food into his bedroom to serve him there (v. 10). Again, she does as she is told—hoping that he will eat and that she can go back home again.

However, this is where an apparently innocent set of circumstances is seen for what it is: a plot designed to sate Amnon's sexual lust. He grabs her and demands, 'Come to bed with me, my sister.' This short sentence reveals the sinful heart of Amnon. Perhaps just the thought of sleeping with his sister, who should be off-limits to him, excites him. Amnon the firstborn prince is used to getting what he wants.

BROTHERLY LOVE?

Up to this point, Tamar has gone along with Amnon's whims, but when immorality is involved, she is willing to stand her ground. It is doubly wrong for them to sleep together, not only because they are not married, but also because they are so closely related. It is on this basis that Tamar begins to plead with Amnon not to 'do this wicked thing' (v. 12). She then appeals to him to see how this act will bring disgrace upon her. Her third plea is that Amnon himself will not be counted among the 'wicked fools in Israel'. When none of these arguments makes any difference to Amnon, Tamar suggests that they appeal to their father to use his kingly powers to enable them to put aside the normal law and be married (v. 13). Sadly, we see that Tamar loses both the verbal and the physical battle. Amnon is unwilling to listen to reason, he is unwilling to consider how his action will affect Tamar and, at this moment in time, he does not even care for his own reputation. He has allowed himself to dwell so much on his sinful desires that this sin has mastered him, and he commits the horrific act on his sister. With his ears deliberately closed to her pleas and reasoning, he uses his greater physical strength and rapes her (v. 14).

THE DECEIVER

It is plain to see how Amnon deceived his father through his pretended illness. He has also clearly deceived his innocent sister, manipulating circumstances so that she is alone with him. But he has also deceived himself. He spoke of being in love with Tamar (v. 4), yet all the time it was simply animal lust. Love would have listened; love would have wanted the best for Tamar; love would have waited until they were married. But his desire is simply for sex, so he rapes her.

The proof of his motivation is seen in the way that, as soon as he has raped her, he hates her with a frightening intensity (v. 15). Does he justify his actions by thinking that her beauty beguiled him and that her compliance with his earlier demands made it too easy? Now he sees the truth of what she has said. Amnon, as well as Tamar, will be banished from respectable society, so again he ignores her pleas and throws her out. Perhaps the awfulness of his action has hit home and he wants to be rid of her in order to forget what he has done.

But, although Tamar is a woman living in a man's world, she refuses to cover over Amnon's sin. She tears those fancy clothes that signified her virginal state and puts ashes on her head (vv. 18–19). This sign of mourning will soon be explained as mourning for the innocence that has been so cruelly taken from her.

We naturally see Tamar as the weaker of the two characters, as she doesn't have the same physical strength as her brother, but in other ways we can see that she is the stronger. Her determination not to cover up what has happened is proof of this. She has been cruelly wronged, but she is not about to allow this sin to be covered up and Amnon to get away with it. Amnon may have succeeded in having her thrown out, with the doors bolted behind her, but he will in due time have to face the consequences of his heinous act.

FOR FURTHER STUDY

1. In Genesis 27, we read of Jacob deceiving his father Isaac so that he would receive his brother's blessing. What were the lasting results of this? What family discord did it cause?

2. Read Genesis 29:15–30 to see how the tables were turned. How did the deceiver himself become deceived? What sort of marriage did he end up with?

TO THINK ABOUT AND DISCUSS

1. Are there times when we are tempted to twist what God has said in his Word because it does not fit in with what we want?

2. Have there been times in your life when how you have behaved wrongly in the past has come back to haunt you, and you have been on the receiving end when others have acted in similarly wrong ways?

12 Brotherly love

2 Samuel 13:20–39

If you are the parent of more than one child, you are likely to have experienced discord between siblings. You may have been accused by one child of favouring another. Each believes that he or she gets the hardest deal. At times, it seems that they can see no good at all in one another. But this sibling rivalry can be replaced by family loyalty. In my family, I see real concern shown by one child to the other when there is illness or some other problem. And, if one feels that the other has been wronged or may be in danger, anxiety is expressed, although not, perhaps, directly to the sibling. However much they may bicker or just ignore each other, there is still usually that family bond which means that they will care for and stick up for each other.

A SAFE HAVEN

As Tamar leaves Amnon's quarters in her distress, she knows just where to go. Weeping and wearing her torn clothes and ashes, she goes to her brother Absalom. Although one brother has abused her badly, she knows that Absalom is a brother to be trusted. The brother and sister obviously have a close relationship.

Straight away, on seeing Tamar in her distress, Absalom recognizes the cause to be Amnon (v. 20). He probably knows that Tamar has gone to Amnon's quarters; he may even have been uneasy about this but unable to do anything, as Tamar has been sent at David's command. He now does his best to comfort her, although I don't imagine she actually received great comfort from his words. To point out that 'he is your brother' would surely only have compounded her distress; she knows this fact well. Also, to say 'Don't take this thing to heart' is almost beyond belief. Tamar has been raped; her virginity has been cruelly taken and the life she has planned is in tatters. Any hopes and dreams of a great wedding celebration followed by the joy of a family of her own have been shattered.

We don't know how Tamar responds to Absalom's clumsy attempts to comfort her. She is a desperate woman in need of a place of safety. In spite of his words, Tamar, desolate and disgraced, recognizes the love and concern Absalom has for her and that he won't turn her away. She finds her safe haven in Absalom's home. Surprisingly, Absalom does not go immediately to 'settle the score' with Amnon. We do not know whether Tamar would feel relieved that there will be no more family trauma, or disappointed that Absalom is not behaving as the avenging protector she expects him to be.

A MEASURED MAN

Absalom is a man who bides his time. He does not rush to confront Amnon at a time when Amnon will be on his guard. Instead, he awaits his opportunity; in fact, he has to wait two whole years. Many times during this period, no doubt, he looks with sadness at Tamar, a woman whose life has been marred by one lust-filled act of selfishness.

Then the opportunity presents itself. After David refuses his invitation to join him at sheep-shearing, Absalom requests that Amnon join him, and David decides to send all his sons to join the party (vv. 24–27). If David feels at all suspicious about Absalom's motives, he also thinks that there is safety in numbers. Absalom's anger against Amnon has not subsided during these intervening years; perhaps his bitterness has even caused it to grow. Knowing that Amnon will take the opportunity to avail himself of the wine that he has provided, Absalom puts his plot into operation. When Amnon is in high spirits from the wine, and therefore not as able to deal with a threat of danger as when he is sober, Absalom's men kill him (vv. 28–29). Perhaps this seems a fitting end for a man who used his physical strength to overcome Tamar.

SADNESS MULTIPLIED

We do not read of David's response to the rape of Tamar, but no doubt he felt great sadness when he heard of it, a sadness probably compounded with a sense of guilt, because he had been drawn into the evil plan. Now a messenger arrives to tell him that Absalom has killed all his sons (v. 30), and David's grief is, understandably, without bounds. Thankfully for David, this message is soon corrected: in fact, only Amnon is dead. What a roller coaster of emotion—from thinking that all his sons are dead to the relief of realizing that only one is dead! But one is still too many. What sadness, to realize that one brother has killed another for the sake of a wronged sister! This is one dysfunctional family! As David and his other sons begin their grieving, Absalom flees (v. 34), no doubt in fear of the king's anger and for his own life.

FOR FURTHER STUDY

1. Read Psalm 5. It was written by David, but it could apply well to Tamar's situation. What does it tell us about God and how he sees evil? What confidence can we have in him when evil is carried out against us?

2. Look at Psalm 34, also written by David. What comfort could this psalm have given to Tamar and others in similar situations?

TO THINK ABOUT AND DISCUSS

1. If a friend of yours experienced a situation similar to that of Tamar, how might you encourage her to start putting her life back together again?

2. Can you think of Christians who, in your lifetime, have gone through tough times but have known God's strengthening through those times?

13 The end of the story?

2 Samuel 14

For three years, Absalom is away from his father, not daring to return. In this chapter, we read that David longs for his son Absalom, yet he makes no effort to bring him back. It takes the intervention of his servant Joab, who employs the services of a wise woman. She speaks to the king in parables until he recognizes that he should allow Absalom back from exile (v. 21). It is then another two years before David and Absalom are reunited (vv. 28–33); sadly, this is only a relatively brief reunion before Absalom starts plotting against his father. It would seem that the years of harbouring bitterness against his brother and his father have done a destructive work in his heart and life.

WHAT ABOUT TAMAR?

This is the end of this part of the story for David and Absalom, but what about Tamar? When we consider all that she has been through, we see what a tough life she has had. Although born a privileged daughter of the king, she has had her innocence and her position snatched away from her by one she should have been able to trust. She has gone to live in Absalom's household, feeling the burden of shame through no fault of her own. During those first two years, perhaps she has begun to settle down, putting aside her girlish hopes and making the best of her situation.

Then she sees things spiral out of control as one brother kills another, bringing more discord into the family. While in one way she is presumably happy that the wrong done to her has been avenged, in another way she must feel a burden of responsibility, because this has been done for her sake. She then sees this loyal brother, who has been eaten up by hate and bitterness, fall out of favour with their father. She must worry about the long-term effect this will have on Absalom, and she is right to do so.

But what about Tamar herself? It would appear that for her, unlike Judah's Tamar and Bathsheba, there is to be no husband who will ease her pain and with whom she will share the joy of children. There is one small, positive note in verse 27: she has a niece named after her. Is this a small way by which Absalom feels that he can ease the pain of her single and childless state? Does she become the doting aunt, delighting in her nieces and nephews? We do not know. But what we do know is that she is part of a dynasty that, though it got much wrong, was part of the purposes of God. In this book we have seen David at his worst; we have had his failings laid bare before us. Yet he is still the one described as 'a man after his [God's] own heart' (1 Samuel 13:14). He is 'commended' in that gallery of faith in Hebrews 11.

We have seen much pain and distress in these five years of Tamar's life. It is around this time that David wrote Psalm 3, expressing his trust in God whatever his circumstances. We can only hope that Tamar shared this same trust in the God who would help her through even the most difficult of circumstances, the one who 'sticks closer than a brother' (Proverbs 18:24).

FOR FURTHER STUDY

1. Read Psalm 3. How does David express his faith and trust in God in spite of the troubles he is facing?

2. Read 2 Corinthians 1:3–11. What positive outcome can our suffering produce? How is this possible?

TO THINK ABOUT AND DISCUSS

1. How can we find comfort in our distress, even in the most traumatic experiences? How can we comfort others in their distress? (See 2 Corinthians 1:3–7.)

2. Having read about these three women, how are you better able to respond to and pray about those who have had similar experiences?

About Day One:

Day One's threefold commitment:

- To be faithful to the Bible, God's inerrant, infallible Word;
- To be relevant to our modern generation;
- To be excellent in our publication standards.

I continue to be thankful for the publications of Day One. They are biblical; they have sound theology; and they are relative to the issues at hand. The material is condensed and manageable while, at the same time, being complete—a challenging balance to find. We are happy in our ministry to make use of these excellent publications.

JOHN MACARTHUR, PASTOR-TEACHER, GRACE COMMUNITY CHURCH, CALIFORNIA

It is a great encouragement to see Day One making such excellent progress. Their publications are always biblical, accessible and attractively produced, with no compromise on quality. Long may their progress continue and increase!

JOHN BLANCHARD, AUTHOR, EVANGELIST AND APOLOGIST

Visit our website for more information and to request a free catalogue of our books.

www.dayone.co.uk

Face2face series

FACE**2**FACE: TAMAR, BATHSHEBA AND TAMAR

FACE**2**FACE: TAMAR, BATHSHEBA AND TAMAR

FACE**2**FACE: TAMAR, BATHSHEBA AND TAMAR

FACE**2**FACE: TAMAR, BATHSHEBA AND TAMAR

FACE**2**FACE: TAMAR, BATHSHEBA AND TAMAR